The Book of Life

Stephen Ridley

BALBOA.
PRESS

A DIVISION OF HAY HOUSE

ISBN: 978-1-4525-5836-3 (sc)
ISBN: 978-1-4525-5837-0 (e)

Balboa Press books may be ordered through booksellers or by contacting:

Balboa Press
A Division of Hay House
1663 Liberty Drive
Bloomington, IN 47403
www.balboapress.com
1-(877) 407-4847

2nd Edition

Printed in the United States of America

Balboa Press rev. date: 10/26/12

THE ONE PROJECT
The Transformation of Human Consciousness

The Father is preparing by His own will
A disciplined people, whom He can fill
With the glory of His presence, His 'I Am,'
Ascending Zion's mountain with the Lamb.

His Book of Life becoming, filled with grace,
Holding forth the Word of Life, to embrace
The whole of this creation until the Light
Has illumined every man. No more night.

Anon.

Contents

Contents

1

Introduction

If this book helps you, please share it with your family and loved ones. Discuss the purpose and meaning together.

Conscious, free will Human Beings have always wondered where they come from and the meaning of their existence. Human *Beings* are soul creations. They are a mirror and reflection of completeness.

Those that choose wisely will return forever to Source. To do this they must be worthy of creation. The Source demands nothing more than this, but nothing less. Selflessness holds the key to unlock the gate.

Human Beings cannot be outside the Universe that created them. Within it, they will realise that they are made from the same energy and purpose. This creative will is connected in all of purpose, direction and across all dimensions.

Energy cannot be controlled for selfish purposes. That is the nature of the Universe. Energy is available to all

Human Beings to manifest love and beauty and nothing more. All else is short lived.

Time appears to govern all, but only the truth is sustainable and without end. That is the nature of truth. Facts are a snapshot of reality, but not reality itself. Reality is a succession of current possibilities, like beads on a thread.

The beads are like facts, deceptive in isolation. Their purpose is not seen until the whole is created. Facts are limited by space, time and short term existence, isolated and potentially misleading views of reality.

The thread is truth, which runs through without end. Only the truth is sustainable. At the core of the thread is *love*. Love is constructive and benevolent, linking each bead through constructive and benevolent possibility.

Any Being that lives outside this sustainable truth cannot be sustained by the Creator environment, neither by the energy from which it is made nor the space within which it temporarily exists as current form.

From the centre of conscious thought, Human Beings can learn to look from the outside in. This is how each Being is seen. Each Human Being has the free will to choose a self-centred or the Universal perspective.

From the centre of selfless actions, Human Beings can either learn to give and share from the inside out, or else take from the outside in. The former is manifested by collaboration; the latter is executed by separation. Separation from energy and all current forms is separation from the Source of Creation.

The free will choice of Human Beings is the path to enlightenment and a return to the Source of Creation. The Source of Creation manifests as Universal connection. It is *no thing*, yet everything.

No thing has many names. It manifests as all and One. Separation is not part of The One's nature. This book will manifest reconnection with The One, the Source of Creation, for all those who choose.

2
Collaboration

The value of collaboration is distinct from any separation. Separation can take many forms.

It can be separation from the nature of true self and Being; it can be separation from other individual Beings and their current form; it can be separation from the process of connection; it can be separation from the Universal mind and intention, which is intended as One and *for* all.

The whole is One. The One has many names but the reality of the whole is the same. These are eternal and infinite space, structure and possibility. Only The One can ordain space.

The Universal Mind, connected and selfless as intended, is the Source of Creation. The possibilities collaborate to construct new possibilities. These are eternal and infinite.

Selfish possibilities, limited in time and space, can only destroy through inversion and reduction. Only positive can create positive. Positive cannot reduce or exclude. That is the meaning of collaboration, created for all and One.

Collaboration is the choice of free will. To choose not to collaborate cannot be sustained in the Universe that is the essence of The One, which is intended to be connected and whole.

3
Constructiveness

Constructiveness and benevolence are morality. Thoughts and actions can only be moral if they are constructive and benevolent. If thoughts and actions are not moral they are meaningless Being, separated from the Source meaning and purpose of Being. Constructiveness is the first pillar of morality. Moral value creates sustainability for *Human* Beings.

Moral values are essential beacons. They underpin creating and creativity. They are both the foundation stones upon which to build and guiding Lights to illuminate the Way. *True* values reconnect Human Beings with the Source of Creation. Only true values, thoughts and actions are sustainable.

Immorality is separation. Amorality is meaningless. Amorality and immorality are not part of Universal intention. Morality cannot be personal or subjective. Destructive thoughts and actions are not sustainable.

Constructiveness is born of Light. It is creating and sharing for others, with others. It is not focussed on self. Constructiveness is Light acting as One.

Constructiveness and benevolence are the two essential cores of moral value. Without them moral value is meaningless. Without moral value, there can be no reconnection. Without the moral values of constructiveness and benevolence, the existence of Human Beings is unsustainable.

4

Benevolence

Benevolence is the second pillar of morality. Without constructiveness the act of benevolence is meaningless. Benevolence is *for* others and *with* others in sharing the outcome.

Sharing starts with the willingness to allow others into one's own life without imposing own or self-view of life as a condition. Benevolence is unconditional.

Sharing creates connection; it creates growth. Sharing creates sufficiency in the community. Sharing enables sufficient for all.

That which is shared is a gift. That which is a gift is revered. Reverence for the gift of sharing creates connection. The connection enables return to the Source. It is a virtuous circle.

Connection with others no matter their circumstances, no matter their past, is essential. Do not judge others for their past and circumstances, which have been unique to them.

The present can be shared through collaborative benevolence, the act of unifying through common values that are giving and inclusive. This act creates unifying circumstances for sharing where The One is all, and all act as a unified One.

This shared view of common circumstances creates the connection and reconnection. With this connected view of benevolence, separation is impossible. This connection is essential for the survival of Human Beings.

5

Commitment

Commit with all your heart towards your heart's desire. The direction gives purpose and the desire the meaning. The desire should be *love* at all times.

Commit all your resources. Do not hold back and commit to winning.

When commitment falters, find inspiration through passion and compassion. This integrity creates *continuity*.

Love like there is no tomorrow; commit like there is no past. Commit to your *love*.

Your love will be where your heart is. Love is your reward. Winning and completion is the result, reconnection, as *One*.

6
Integrity

Integrity creates continuity.

Integrity is honouring your word, intending to be true to what you say.

With Light in your heart, trust how you feel. Be true to the values. Honour your word.

Be resilient, with hope and promise in your heart. Stay with love, within the Light. Be faithful to the end.

The choice is yours and no other's, in step with the Universe. The choice is continuous.

7
Passion

Passion is the intensity of desire. It creates resilience in the face of difficulty or antagonism on the Way to finding the truth. Passion is the fire of the soul. It creates the Light and love within. Passion gives the motivation to continue the journey with integrity.

Passion can be felt. It is the heart and soul of *Being*. The feeling gives rise to thoughts of action. Passion is personal striving: desire towards the truth, the meaning and the goal; striving to your heart's desire, which is born of love.

Passion manifests conscious thinking that becomes the Way of Being. When passion wavers the Way of Being consciously takes over until the passion reappears. Conscious thinking is the holding ground. Passion is the power of motivation, to move and realise the goal.

Follow your heart's desire based on *love*. This is where you will find the *truth*. Passion is in the heart, along with the courage of a lion. Passion will sustain.

The quest will never be easy. There is no easy path, no easy Way. Do not let the uneven path or rocky terrain deter you from the goal. The *design* of the Way is to *learn, grow and share.*

The quest is by you, but not for you. The quest will be known when truth is felt, with purity in heart and with consciousness of mind. With trust and faith the goal will be known and realised.

Climb where you must, even if the path is difficult and seems impossible. Descend where you must, when you must, to find the path again. There are many paths that arrive at the same place, but the direction is the same. Share the known journey and what is learned for the benefit of others.

When the bedrock is found the real quest will start. With it will be many unturned stones, masking the true undertaking which is for the rest of your days. Do not leave any of the stones unturned, even if the experience is collapse. Collapse is short lived. With passion, the truth will be uncovered and the learning fulfilled. If the quest or understanding is not clear or elusive, return another day.

Be prepared for physiological and psychological change, but do not risk harm this day to the point of not being able to continue, to return and learn. There are many layers and many discoveries.

Take heart on the journey back, for that gives the passion, courage and will to return and complete the journey. Every journey is unique. All will be revealed with trust and faith. Love *will* be found.

8

Compassion

Love is for *giving*. Forgiveness heals wounds. Compassion is the art of forgiveness.

Give love without reserve, without reason and without doubt. The act of forgiveness heals the soul. Past hurts will dissolve.

Compassion is Universal, for all. Removal of doubt creates the space for healing wounds between two souls. The healing is personal, between two souls. Seeing another as one-self makes separation disappear. This makes a lack of forgiveness impossible.

Remember that another's pain is not yours, but act and feel as though it was. Recognition and the reconnection will remove pain, for both. The Universal act of forgiveness creates the space for all and One. The result is an act for The One and reconnection with the Source of Creation.

9

Excellence

Excellence has no boundaries or limits. It creates the space for all possibility with nothing, from *no thing*.

True excellence is built with value, for value. It is collaborative, constructive and benevolent. Excellence is resilient, continuous and virtuous. Excellence needs personal integrity.

The value of sharing is honoured through collaborative teaching and learning. Sharing makes excellence a Way of Being. True excellence continuously thinks, acts, learns and teaches.

Lead by example. Be true to your heart. True leaders, those worthy of following, *serve* their followers. Teach and encourage others to act for others and without fear. Excel without reason, excuse or constraint. Compete with one-self before others.

Excel to persevere with strength of a bull, intend with the purity of an angel and have the courage and heart of a lion. Excellence rises and soars on the wings of an eagle. It spirals upwards until the goal is reached.

Excellence is Universal intent.

10

Choice and Free Will

Human Beings have free will. The free will is choice. The choice has two paths. There is no other choice. The One is Light. The other is separation and desolation.

The One is *sharing*, *giving* and *love*. It creates love, and life. It is *no thing* and yet everything. The other creates fear, hatred, jealousy, anger and rejection. The One is hope. The other is despair. The One embraces love and has no fear. The other rejects love. Love is all and One, together, with no separation from another.

Free will and destiny are One. Free will is the archer. Destiny is the flight of the arrow. Connection is seeing and accepting both. Free will is the horseman. Destiny is the wind in the hair. They are One. In choosing the other the wind will redirect the arrow onto the unworthy horseman. Free will is the choice. There is no other choice.

11
Cause and Effect

Cause and effect are observations of temporary form within the mind of Human Beings.

Tubular bells hanging in straight lines, like a planted avenue in all directions. A bell is moved until it touches and moves the others. The others move until all are One, moving each other. Human Beings falsely perceive the first move.

There is no beginning. There is no end. That is eternity. Eternity is *no thing*. It extends beyond the reach and perception of most. That is infinity.

Human Beings can perceive infinity beyond the reach. It is a snapshot of the whole, the eternal. The snapshot is the *here and now*. The whole, the here and now, is One. The One is the cause. The effect is the choice, the free will to choose.

Time distorts the perception and creates the paradox. Time creates the perception of space for making the choice. If Light is chosen, the effect is increased Light. Light is cause and effect, the will of The One.

The Light and One create possibility without limit. Without limit or boundary there can be no separation. Connection and *One-ness* is completion.

Thought and action give rise to creation, and give rise the will of The One. Time, cause and effect are the technologies of Human Beings to help understand and manifest the Universal will.

12

Meaning

Direction gives the purpose; desire gives the meaning. The meaning and purpose are One.

Purpose cannot be found in individual things because they are isolated and separated in a perceived chain of cause and effect. Individual things are transitory towards the purpose. The purpose is a *sustainable* truth.

Purpose is growth, with conscious free will and choice, towards The One.

Human Beings with value are *within* the Universal intention to grow. Values give the direction and foundation for truth. Growth is purpose, as individuals and collaboratively, as One and for The One. The meaning is learning. The purpose is growth.

Love *gives* meaning. It is given without condition. Love is *for giving*, without limit or end. It has always been. Love is infinite and eternal.

Souls with purpose and meaning will *grow* in love. The wise will learn. Enlightened souls live in love, for love. Only enlightened souls in the value of The One are sustainable at the end of days. The One does not choose. One-self is the creation of individual Being, with individual choice to reconnect with the Source of Creation.

13

Light and Shadow

That which is pure needs no distinction. Love needs no opposite. Love is Light. Light needs no opposite.

Shadow is the true distinction of Light. Light can be seen from within shadow when shadows are cast. Shadow indicates the direction of the Light. Light casts shadows to help show the Way.

Shadows help understanding. Experience of shadows creates wisdom, the Way back to Universal truth. The shadow is not the end. The end is not the end. The shadows are the beginning of an enlightened journey, to rediscover the Light and live in the Light to end of days.

Wisdom understands Light and shadow. This is the Way of enlightenment and the return to Universal Source.

14

Adjustment

Opinion can only give a limited viewpoint based on the perceptions of the Human mind, generated from within the Human mind's understanding of reality. Opinions and understanding *within* the temporal world are based on assumption, with gaps in knowledge. They are diverse and transient. They are not the truth.

Belief in itself is incomplete. Belief is not the same as knowing the stepping stones across the river or of the nature of the river-bank beyond. Belief, personal sacrifice, passion and compassion are the essence of faith. They are all essential ingredients of faith. All are tested through conscious thinking and action. Faith is tested through continual choice.

Knowledge, the gift of *knowing*, has no reliance upon assumptions. It requires complete faith and surrender of the self to access the Gate.

Conscious thinking and action within Universal value, and a desire for connection with The One, gives access to an understanding of knowledge, the knowing of *spirit* that connects all and One.

Spirit is of energy. Knowing of spirit within each Human Being gives access to recognition of the soul within other Human Beings and of the soul and spirit of and within *all other sentient Beings.*

Spirit is the action within each Being, from and for each soul. Each soul acts for another through spirit and Universal connection and intention.

Soul is the core of Being. Spirit is the energy of action. It is spirit that creates true connection, not the mind.

The mind is the tool, the mechanism, to recognise and understand the process. The mind will deceive if the mind thinks it created itself. The mind cannot be made from anything less or more than the energy of the Universe. Consciousness is energy observing its own form.

Enlightened Human Beings will adjust and move from the mind, towards understanding, on to *knowledge through spirit.* The enlightened with knowledge will recognise end of days and choose to return to the Source of Creation. They will recognise truth and understand the transformation for others. Transformation towards Source is conversion to *knowing.*

Trust the knowing of the enlightened. The enlightened are not leaders for the self. Self- declaration is a contradiction. True leaders will be for One and all, leaders serving followers.

15
Truth

The truth is eternal and infinite. It is Universal. Only the truth is sustainable.

Immoral thoughts and actions are created of mind, from within the mind. Amorality is meaningless.

Darkness descends and intrudes without reference. Light finds its Way through reflection. Light always finds a Way to illuminate the dark. Without Light there is no Way to see and *know* reality. *Knowing* is therefore enlightenment.

Light does not work in part. Light is inclusive. Constructiveness is inclusive, expansive, dynamic, positive and ceaseless. Constructiveness and benevolence as One are truths, sustainable and virtuous. Truths are known because they are sustainable. Truths sustain life, through life.

Moral action is collaborative, the connection of spirit. Sharing with others creates a Way of Being that is not focussed on self. This action creates knowing of morality. Knowing transforms the mind and the Way of Being.

Understanding of constructiveness and benevolence breaks immorality within the mind. Constructive and benevolent actions break immorality of results. These core values are *virtuous circles*, upward spirals returning to the Source of Creation.

Only the truth can be sustainable. A virtuous circle is sustainable because it has neither a beginning nor an end, like a circle. That is infinity and eternity, the Universe. Linear thinking is false because it assumes the opposite. Assumptions are gaps in knowledge. Linear thinking is based on assumptions within the Human mind.

The Universal truth is that love is creation. Creation is love. Love is the grail. The chalice is the cup of love, the shape of true love and happiness. It cannot be found in one-self or all until it is found within The One.

16
Reality

Reality is perceived through open mind working in the present moment. The unconscious mind is filled with self-generated thoughts of the past and future. The power of the here and now wills the open, conscious mind without interference and noise of the unconscious mind. Fear, hate, jealousy and anger are generated from within the unconscious mind.

The unconscious mind must be closed to deception to perceive reality and truth. The gate to understanding can only be opened by conscious surrender of the self will.

Reality is like the honeycomb of a honey bee. The structure can be seen or felt, but without the space within the structure there can be no structure. The bee sees both, the structure and the space. The structure creates the house. The space provides the room for possibility and creation.

Understanding which was created first is based on perspective, looking from the outside in, followed by perception, looking from the inside out. This sequence helps understanding.

The structure cannot be created before the space. The space creates the dimension for the structure. The structure can then be built upon strong foundations and values created by and within the space. The structure is formed according to the benefits and values of the Creator. These can be selfish and short lived, or connected to The One and for all. The Universal will is always connected and sustainable.

The honey bee also sees beyond the structure and the space. It sees space as the basis for creation within it. This is the true nature of reality: the space, the structure and the possibility within. Human Beings have the free will to decide which possibility to create, which path to choose, leading to connection or separation. Separation is not sustainable. Honey bees are connected to both the honeycomb and one another. They are connected to their environment.

Possibility can only last as a sustainable truth governed by the Universe. Reality is truth. So which is real: That which is transient or that which is eternal? That is the essence of the journey, the quest and the choice, the path to transformation and enlightenment.

17

Transformation

Only the here and now exists for Human Beings, here and now.

The past is a recall of facts as they *were*, within the Human mind, within the Human perception of time. Past facts give experience and the basis for learning, to provide information for new creation as it is *now*, from this moment on. Possibility for the future can only be created within the here and now.

The future is no more and no less than anticipation of how the facts might be within the realm of infinite possibility. Only within the here and now can transformation be found. Transformation is a learning process.

Transformation is the key to move from understanding facts of current form to knowledge of infinite possibility. This is creation. The form or matter of facts is a snapshot of reality. It is transient until the new form is created. The energy of truth is eternal. Form is the construct of energy. Dynamic energy is created by space.

Insecurity is rooted in thoughts about the past or projections into the future. The future is *unknowable* without transformation. The now has no insecurity. Positivity creates positivity. Positive thoughts and actions in the here and now create security, both now and as future possibility.

Consciousness is energy observing its own form. Observing own thinking in the here and now changes the perspective of the Human mind. All things can disappear through perspective from within the here and now, including hate, fear, anger, jealousy and conflict. If Human Beings are secure within one-self, nothing that any other Being does makes it otherwise.

Absolutes are symbols describing the reach of Human thought. All reality, the sum of all possibilities, is relative to perspective. Humans are bounded Beings within a self-centred perception of reality. Knowledge of the infinite is impossible for any bounded Being. Temporary form and facts are created by and bounded within reality. Self-centred perspective prevents Human knowledge of the infinite and eternal, the sum of all possibilities.

Only unselfish and unbounded thought and action can realise this knowledge. Living in the here and now, with selflessness, activates the process. These are the keys to transformation and reconnection with Source.

Reconnection with Source connects the possibility for more transformation in others. The change in Human consciousness is the key to survival within the Universe that created this possibility. This possibility ensures return to Source and understanding of true love and happiness within the temporal world.

This is the intention of all and One, the return of the garden as intended for growth of spirit, soul and connection with One-another.

18
A New Order

The world will change.

The second comes when Human Beings transform. This is the new level of Human consciousness. Human consciousness will transform to a higher plane.

Space creates the dimension; energy creates the delivery; form creates the means; desire creates the meaning; values are the direction and create the Light along the Way, continuous and sustainable. The soul is preserved within the Universal intent of value.

The spirit of doing is fulfilment of the energy and intent. It connects the space of The One with the form of reality. The purpose of reality is the truth, which is sustainable. Fulfilment is connection and reconnection with The One.

The garden will return. Separation will cease. This is Universal intention, the intention of The One.

Choose wisely. The choice is for you and no other. Your choice is your life, your meaning and your purpose.

It is not enough to be good with or kind to some people and still judge others. Each person is another Being, exactly the same as another, no matter how they live their life. That is their journey, not for self to judge. Each Human Being should be treated as though they are exactly the same.

Nor is it enough to be humanitarian. There are other sentient beings on Earth that Human Beings must connect with. Human Beings must connect with and respect all forms of Being.

The people who surrender; those who treat all others as though themselves; those who love and honour community; those who revere the essence in all objects; those who perceive emotional and spiritual connection in all things; those who see the Way; those who live in the values of the *common good*: all these will receive the Light, returning Heaven to Earth, and Earth to Heaven.

The key words to understand are caring, sharing, giving and love. Share this book with those that you love. Be prepared for change and sharing. Love is the space.

Love is creation. It manifests through belief, personal sacrifice, passion and compassion. *Creation is love. One is Love. Love is One.*

Stay faithful to the end, your heart's desire fulfilled.

Love and peace be with you, the will of The One.

Printed in the United States
By Bookmasters